Lea
Tropical

With 12 Stickers

Jan Sovak

DOVER PUBLICATIONS
Garden City, New York

Introduction

In this little book you'll learn about some of the world's most dazzling fish. They live in and near coral reefs, which thrive in warm, tropical waters north and south of the equator. As you read about each amazing creature, you will be able to illustrate its page with a colorful sticker portrait that will help the fish come alive in your imagination.

Queen Angelfish

The young queen angelfish has vertical bars on its body; the adult is iridescent yellow and blue. A black spot on the top of its head makes it appear to be wearing a crown. The queen angelfish is found in the coral reefs and shallow waters of the Florida Keys, the Bahamas, and the Gulf of Mexico. The queen angelfish prefers a diet of sponges.

Blue-Striped Grunt

The blue-striped grunt is named for the noise it makes when it grinds together its strong throat muscles, which act as teeth. Found in shallow water near the shore, these fish form schools when in deep water along reefs. The blue-striped grunt lives in Florida and the Bahamas as well as the Caribbean, as far south as Brazil. It eats mostly shrimp.

Coney

With small spots on its body that are usually blue, the coney's background color ranges from golden yellow to red and brown. When it is excited, the bottom of its body may become almost white, with its top turning very dark. Coneys are found from South Carolina to the Gulf of Mexico and the Caribbean. They take in small fish and crustaceans rapidly, eating them whole.

Puffer

When alarmed or disturbed, the puffer balloons up to several times its normal size by drawing in water or air. Living among coral reefs that are close to the shore in warm, mostly saltwater regions around the globe, the puffer is a poisonous fish that can kill its prey using its toxin and its four large teeth.

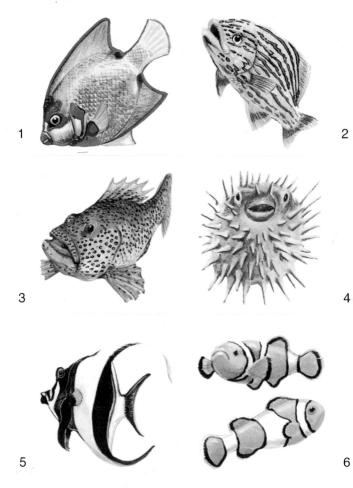

1

2

3

4

5

6

AFTER ALL THE STICKERS HAVE BEEN PLACED IN THE CORRECT SPACES,
PLEASE GENTLY REMOVE AND DISCARD THESE TWO PAGES.

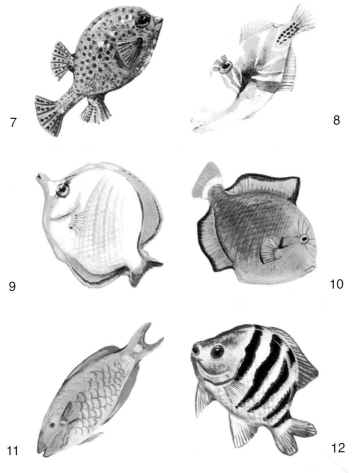

7

8

9

10

11

12

AFTER ALL THE STICKERS HAVE BEEN PLACED IN THE CORRECT ⸗
PLEASE GENTLY REMOVE AND DISCARD THESE TWO PAGES.

Moorish Idol

Its black, white, and pale yellow
stripes make the Moorish idol one of
the most striking of the small reef fish.
It camouflages itself at night by
darkening its body to black. Living on
deepwater coral reefs, it is often visible
in shallow waters. The Moorish idol
can be found in tropical seas near
East Africa, Micronesia, Japan,
Hawaii, and Mexico's Pacific coast.
It feeds on sponges as well as other
invertebrates.

Clown Fish

Clown fish live within the poisonous tentacles of the giant sea anemone, protecting it from predators. In exchange, clown fish, which seem to be immune to the sea anemone's poison, clean the sea anemone, although scientists are not sure how this partnership works. These fish live in the Indian and Pacific oceans and the Great Barrier Reef, eating algae and zooplankton.

Spotted Trunkfish

In addition to a body enclosed in an armor of bony plates, the spotted trunkfish, when it's threatened, secretes a substance poisonous enough to kill another fish, including sharks. Its diet includes algae, crustaceans, sea urchins, and marine plants. Trunkfish live in the Pacific, Atlantic, and Indian oceans, as well as in waters from Florida to Cape Cod.

Picasso Triggerfish

The Picasso triggerfish can watch an intruder with one eye while using the other to search for a crevice to hide in. Dramatically colored and patterned, the Picasso triggerfish has tough skin that looks as if it has been painted, which explains the "Picasso" in its name. It lives in the Indo-Pacific region.

Yellowhead Butterfly Fish

Yellowhead butterfly fish, one of a hundred known species of butterfly fish, live in pairs. If they become separated, one swims to the highest nearby coral head and waits for the other to find it. They live in the Indian Ocean from the East African coast to Sri Lanka, off the southern tip of India. Yellowhead butterfly fish use their hairlike teeth to feed on coral polyps.

Orange Band Surgeonfish

All surgeonfish have retractable spines that are razor-sharp. Effective weapons for slashing rivals, these spines can also be dangerous to humans. The snouts of these fish taper into small mouths, which they use to scrape food from coral. The orange band surgeonfish is found in the Indian and Pacific oceans in tropical and subtropical waters ranging from western Australia to Hawaii.

Stoplight Parrotfish

With its teeth fused into a strong beak much like that of a parrot, the stoplight parrotfish scrapes algae from coral, sometimes damaging the reef. Before swallowing, it grinds up the coral with teeth that it has in its throat. It also grazes on sponges. The parrotfish is common in West Indian coral reefs as well as Florida and Brazil.

Sergeant Major

Groups of 8 to 10 sergeant majors, each up to 1 inch long, travel and feed together on shallow reefs. Larger sergeant majors live in tropical waters along the northeastern and eastern coasts of the Atlantic Ocean and have a diet that includes algae, crustaceans, zooplankton, and small fish.